D0454434

I Notice Animals in Fall

by Mari Schuh

Lerner Publications ◆ Minneapolis

LERNER

SOURCE™

Expand learning beyond the printed book. Download free, complementary educational resources for this book from our website, www.lernerresource.com.

Copyright © 2017 by Lerner Publishing Group, Inc.

All rights reserved. International copyright secured. No part of this book may be reproduced, stored in a retrieval system, or transmitted in any form or by any means—electronic, mechanical, photocopying, recording, or otherwise—without the prior written permission of Lerner Publishing Group, Inc., except for the inclusion of brief quotations in an acknowledged review.

The images in this book are used with the permission of: © Design Pics Inc/Alamy, p. 4; © Josef Pittner/Shutterstock.com, pp. 5, 9; © kamilpetran/Shutterstock.com, p. 6; © iStockphoto.com/Kim_Schott, p. 7; © Peter Wey/Shutterstock.com, p. 8; © iStockphoto.com/AdShooter, p. 10; © MVPhoto/Shutterstock.com, p. 11; © solarseven/Shutterstock.com, p. 12; © Brian Guest/Shutterstock.com, p. 13; © JHVEPhoto/Shutterstock.com, p. 14; © Nils Prause/Shutterstock.com, p. 15; © Daniel Gale/Shutterstock.com, p. 16; © iStockphoto.com/Cucu Remus, p. 17; © iStockphoto.com/Dieter Meyrl, p. 18; © Breck P. Kent/Animals Animals/Earth Sciences, p. 19; © John A. Anderson/Shutterstock.com, p. 20; © Michael Francis Photography/Animals Animals, p. 21; © kospet/Shutterstock.com, p. 22.
Front cover: © iStockphoto.com/Chris Hepburn.

Main body text set in ITC Avant Garde Gothic Std Medium 21/25.
Typeface provided by International Typeface Corp.

Lerner Publications Company
A division of Lerner Publishing Group, Inc.
241 First Avenue North
Minneapolis, MN 55401 USA

For reading levels and more information, look up this title at www.lernerbooks.com.

Library of Congress Cataloging-in-Publication Data

Schuh, Mari C., 1975– author.
   I notice animals in fall / by Mari Schuh.
      pages cm. — (First step nonfiction. Observing fall)
   Audience: Ages 5–8.
   Audience: K to grade 3.
   Summary: "This title describes the ways in which animals adapt and get ready for winter during the fall. Readers will learn to observe the world around them as well as to spot signs of seasonal changes in nature"— Provided by publisher.
   ISBN 978-1-5124-0792-1 (lb : alk. paper) — ISBN 978-1-5124-1213-0 (pb : alk. paper) — ISBN 978-1-5124-0994-9 (eb pdf)
   1. Animal behavior—Juvenile literature. 2. Animal migration—Juvenile literature. 3. Autumn—Juvenile literature. I. Title.
   QL751.5.S384 2016
   591.5—dc23   2015036032

Manufactured in the United States of America
1 – CG – 7/15/16

Table of Contents

Animals Get Ready

Animals are busy in the fall. They are getting ready for winter.

Food is hard to
find in the snow.

Soon it will be cold.
It may snow.

Squirrels gather and save nuts. They will eat them later.

Groundhogs eat more food.
They won't eat all winter.

Animals Change

Some animals **adapt**
in the fall.

They get ready for the cold weather.

Deer grow thicker fur.
It keeps them warm.

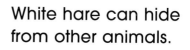
White hare can hide
from other animals.

Brown snowshoe hare
turn white. They will
match the snow.

11

Animals Move

Some animals **migrate** in the fall. They move to warmer places.

Geese fly south for the winter. Together, they form a V-shape.

Monarch butterflies fly to
Mexico and California.
They fly hundreds of miles.

Caribou move after a
snowstorm. They go to
places with less snow.

Animals Sleep

Some animals find places to **hibernate**.

Animals that hibernate spend winter in a very deep sleep.

Bats sleep upside down in dark caves.

Bears sleep in warm dens.

Chipmunks sleep
underground.

Chipmunks sleep in
deep **burrows**.

Insects hide in old logs.

Mud keeps turtles warm.

Turtles crawl into thick mud.

How is this animal getting ready for winter?